FAT
CATS

FAT CATS

KAT SCRATCHING

amber
BOOKS

Published by
Amber Books Ltd
74–77 White Lion Street
London
N1 9PF
United Kingdom
www.amberbooks.co.uk
Appstore: itunes.com/apps/amberbooksltd
Facebook: www.facebook.com/amberbooks
Twitter: @amberbooks

ISBN: 978-1-78274-429-0

Project Editor: Sarah Uttridge
Designer: Rick Fawcett
Picture Research: Terry Forshaw

Printed in China

Picture Credits
Depositphotos: 6 left & right (A Dog's Life Photography), 6 centre top (Denis Mart), 6 centre bottom (Feedough), 8 background (Chen Chien Hung), 8 bottom (Veda Gonzalez), 10 (Funny Cats), 12 (Kuban Girl), 16 (Funny Cats), 18 top (van der Steen Fotografie), 18 bottom (Mara Zemgaliete), 22 (Artem Povarov), 24 right (Pelana), 26 (Sergey Rasulov), 28 left (Ermolaev Alexandr Alexandrovich), 28 top right (kontur-vid), 28 middle right (Hypermania Images), 28 bottom right (kontur-vid), 30 (A Dog's Life Photography), 32 (Sergey Rasulov), 34 (Veda Gonzalez), 36 (Seven2812), 38 right (Lusoimages), 44 (Alexei Chernitevich), 58 (Rommel Canlas), 62 (Funny Cats), 66 (Eleonora Vatel), 68 (GooDween), 70 left (Belchonock), 70 centre (Emmanuelle Bonzami), 72 (Belchonock), 76 (Cris Kelly), 80 (Belchonock), 84 (Svetlana Valyiskaya), 86 (Oxygen2608), 88 (Ezarubina), 90 background (Herb Allgaier), 90 centre (Life On White), 92 (Kvkrillov), 94 (Sergey Rasulov), 96 (Sergey Rasulov)
Dreamstime: 14 (Mateisavin), 20 (Sergey Rasulov), 24 left (Violka08), 38 left (Feng Yu), 40 (Amenic181), 42 (Slovegrove), 46 (Sergey Rasulov), 48 (Isselee), 50 (Vanoa2), 52 (Sergey Rasulov), 54 (Marilyn Gould), 56 (Kristina Sorokina), 60 (Sergey Rasulov), 64 (Kuban Girl), 70 background (Kutt Niinepuu), 74 (S-dmit), 78 (Katarinaelena), 82 (Mik122)

Contents

Partying Like it's an 1869

"Recession? Is that a new perfume or a vodka? Either way, it tastes fine to me."

High Spirits

In 2011, a London hedge-fund owner spent more than $100,000 (£71,000) on a Christmas party for just nine members of staff. Most of the cash went on 24 bottles of Cîroc Ultra Premium vodka, which came to a total of $64,000 (£44,400). The party at the Rose Club, where regulars include George Clooney and Naomi Campbell, ended with the hedge-fund owner tipping the waitress $15,000 (£10,000). A spokesperson for the club said, "The customer, who is one of our regulars, just wanted to give his team an unforgettable Christmas party.

Fare Dodging's the Ticket

"Dogs must be kept on a leash, but it doesn't say anything about cats. So I travel freely—and for free."

Cat in the Rat Race

A Porsche-driving commuter who dodged the fare on his 53-mile train journey to London for five years managed to escape jail by returning the money—and more—once his scam was discovered. Jonathan Burrows, a director at the asset-management firm BlackRock, quickly paid back $62,000 (£43,000) in 2014, which was what he would have owed if he'd only ever bought costly single tickets for his journeys. But when the Financial Conduct Authority heard of his cheating, Burrows, who owned mortgage-free properties totaling $5.7 million (£3.9 million), didn't wait for his employer's reaction. He resigned.

Gangster Bankers

"What can I say? I'm too big to jail."

In the Laundering Basket

Although it acknowledged failures that allowed Mexico's Sinaloa cartel to launder hundreds of millions of dollars through its accounts, British-based bank HSBC received just a slap on the paw and no criminal charges for its sins in 2013. The bank was forced to pay $1.9 billion (£1.3 billion) only because, as U.S. Assistant Attorney General Lanny Breuer said, criminal charges "would almost certainly have lost HSBC its banking license in the U.S., the future of the institution would have been under threat and the entire banking system would have been destabilized."

Feline Good

"Any place in the sun will do for me—as long as it's a tax shelter."

A Mean Average

Within 48 hours of returning to work at the beginning of 2016, top executives in London would already have earned more than the $40,068 (£27,645) average annual salary of a British worker, according to a study by the High Pay Centre (a British think tank). Chief executives working for the largest 100 companies listed on the London Stock Exchange were paid an average $7.1 million (£4.96 million) a year in 2014.

House Trained

"An Englishman's home is his castle. Actually, my home really is a castle, while yours is more like a doghouse."

Domesticated Dividends

Earls, barons, viscounts, and lords are among a group of landlords taking billions from the British state through housing benefits paid on behalf of poorer tenants. As much as $33 billion (£22.8 billion) of taxpayers' cash goes toward subsidizing the rent of 1.65 million private properties in Britain. West Berkshire Council paid a whopping $907,000 (£626,000) to Richard Benyon, the nation's richest MP, who owns 300 houses.

Liquidity Puss

"I can assure you, officer, I'm clean."

Fat Cat Marks Territory

Dennis Kozlowski once spent $6,000 (£4,140) on shower curtains, owned paintings by Renoir and Monet, and at a party had an ice sculpture of Michelangelo's *David* that urinated vodka. As head of security systems manufacturer Tyco International, he was celebrated for taking the firm to multinational status. However, all that changed when, in 2005, he was found to have stolen millions from the company through giving himself unauthorized bonuses, abusing corporate loan programs, and falsifying records. On his release, he referred to prison as "the gated community I used to live in."

*Cat*holic Tastes

"I'm the original Cat in the Hat."

Cardinal Sin

Having been tasked by Pope Francis with examining the Church's finances, Cardinal George Pell announced in 2014 that he could save money for the Church. Unfortunately, the following year, it was reported in the Italian magazine *L'Espresso* that the Cardinal himself had spent $570,000 (£393,000) on luxury items, such as lavish furniture for his apartment in Rome and $15,810 (£10,906) a month on a *purr*sonal assistant. The Vatican condemned the leaking of the documents but did not deny their authenticity.

Cat on the Fiddle

"For me, soccer is a game of two halves—one on the field—the second in the *petit*entiary."

Cat on the Fiddle

Rotund, bewhiskered, and keen on birds—that certainly sounds feline. However, Chuck Blazer, a former *Fédération Internationale de Football Association* (FIFA) power broker of American soccer, earns his place among these pages for money laundering, income tax evasion, wire fraud, and racketeering. Blazer, who kept eclectus parrots, boasted about his high life on his blog, which featured photographs of him alongside Bill Clinton, Nelson Mandela, and Prince William, as well as a couple of Miss Universes. In 2013, he pleaded guilty to the charges against him.

In the Laptop of Luxury

"Bernie Madoff? He's the guy who *made off* with all his investors' money, right?"

Federal Feline Felon

In 2009, Bernie Madoff pleaded guilty to 11 federal felonies, including securities fraud and money laundering. He had defrauded his clients of almost $65 billion (£44.8 billion) in the largest Ponzi scheme in history. He was sentenced to 150 years in jail, admitting he had never made any legitimate investments with his clients' money. Instead, he simply deposited the money into his personal business account, and when his customers asked for withdrawals, he paid them out of that.

Investment Op*paw*tunities

"It was a golden opportunity—just for me, not you. And not actually involving any gold."

Fool's Gold

In October 1995, Bre-X Minerals Ltd., based in Calgary, Canada, announced that gold had been discovered in land it owned in Busang, Indonesia. The company's market value soared to CAD $6 billion ($4.6 billion or £3.2 billion), various Canadian pension funds invested in the company, and all seemed well . . . until it was revealed two years later that there was no gold in Busang. The geological records reporting gold finds had simply been falsified. Shares were frantically sold, lawsuits followed, and the Ontario Teachers' Pension Plan alone lost CAD $100 million (£52.5 million) in the investment.

Catcalling

"Hello, this is WorldCon—excuse me—I mean, World*Com*."

In the Kitty

WorldCom was a U.S. telecom company that aggressively bought up smaller firms in the 1990s. When the tech bubble burst in 2000, the thread of WorldCom's con began to unravel: The company had been artificially inflating its assets by $11 billion (£7.6 billion), and in 2002, it filed for Chapter 11 bankruptcy protection. Its chief executive, Bernard Ebbers, was convicted of fraud in 2005 and is currently serving a 25-year sentence.

Three Strokes and You're Out

"There's no way cats can understand the rules of cricket—it's a team game."

Fouling Play

In 2008, the England and Wales Cricket Board signed a five-year deal with Texan billionaire Allen Stanford, who promised to inject millions into English cricket. However, those millions were merely part of an investment scam in which his Antigua-based Stanford International Bank was selling $11.5 billion (£7.9 billion) worth of "certificates of deposit" that promised investors extraordinarily generous returns. Of course, it was too good to be true; he was simply spending investors' money. Arrested in Virginia in 2009, Stanford was found guilty of fraud and sentenced to 110 years in jail.

A Furball Too Far

"I'm a princess. Of course, I'm accustomed to life at court—just not a court of law."

Those Taxing Tax Returns

In 2016, Princess Cristina of Spain became the first member of the Spanish royal family in modern times to be put on trial. She was charged with failing to declare taxes on personal expenses paid by a real estate company that she owned with her husband, Inaki Urdangarin. If convicted, the princess faces a jail term of up to eight years. Urdangarin, an Olympic handball medalist turned executive, faces the more serious charges of embezzlement, influence peddling, forgery, and money laundering.

Selfie *Paw*traits

"Cats are trendsetters. That's why fashion shows have catwalks."

Puss in Boots
London-based glamor-pusses Leyla and Arzu Aliyeva, daughters of Azerbaijan's President Ilham Aliyev, are believed to share a property portfolio of more than $72 million (£50 million). In 2016, the Panama Papers revealed that the sisters also had financial stakes in an Azerbaijan gold-mining firm and in the country's largest cell-phone business.

Doing It *Fur* Charity

"Charity begins at home—my home."

For a Good Paws

When you give money to charity, you do so in the belief that it's going to a good cause. And as charity bosses will tell you, their salary is definitely a worthwhile cause. In 2014, it was revealed that a top employee of the Britain-based charity Save the Children was earning $339,000 (£234,000) a year, and another six members of staff were earning more than $145,000 (£100,000) each. Their children would be provided for.

Cat That Got the Cream

"What can I tell you? The workplace is just like milk—the cream rises to the top."

A-Whey with You

The mood soured at British milk producer Dairy Crest in 2015 when it was announced that 3,000 staff were to receive what was described as a "miserly" pay increase while chief executive Mark Allen would be lapping up a $1.74 million (£1.2 million) bonus on top of a salary that was already believed to be around $1.85 million (£1.28 million).

Cat Denies Feathering Nest

"Me? Excessive? Butter wouldn't melt on my paws."

Top Cat

Who earns more: the Prime Minister of Great Britain, the head of Oxfam, or the boss of an animal welfare charity in Scotland? Yes, of course, in 2014, Stuart Earley of the Scottish Society for Prevention of Cruelty to Animals (SSPCA) earned $313,530 (£216,320)—more than the head of Oxfam and $95,000 (£66,000) more than Prime Minister David Cameron. Amid accusations that he's the fattest cat, Earley defended his pay, arguing that it was justified by the improved results achieved under his leadership.

Bum Notes

"Would it kill you to give me just a little ap*paws*?"

Bringing Discord to Harmony

Hired to look after the finances of the London Philharmonic Orchestra, Cameron Poole instead siphoned off $936,000 (£645,000) to pay for renovations on his home, exotic vacations, and artworks worth tens of thousands of dollars. Poole used company credit cards for his personal purchases and then concealed those payments by making false entries on the orchestra's accounting system. His actions were only discovered after an internal audit. In 2010, he was jailed for four years.

Catnip and Tuck

"Give me a break, this is my first vacation all week."

Playing Cat and House

The financial manager of a warehousing and logistics company stole $2.2 million (£1.5 million) from her employer, spending the money on such essentials as cosmetic surgery, luxury vacations, and an apartment for one of her daughters. Wendy Nichols, who worked for Logistex, Northamptonshire, Great Britain, was caught when a colleague noticed a financial irregularity. She pleaded guilty in court and in 2013 received more than a five-year sentence.

*Purr*sonal Finance

"I always insist on counting the pennies, whoever's pennies they are."

Expensive Expenses

A secretary working for the British Ministry of Defence was jailed for 22 months after it was discovered that she had swindled her employer out of $144,000 (£99,000) through false expense reports and forged e-mails. Yasmin Disney, 25, spent the money on an Audi TT sports car as well as a car for her boyfriend, luxury vacations, designer handbags, jewelry, and gadgets.

The Great Rock & Roll Swindle

"I like musicals—*Cats* is a favorite—and hip-hop is fine, but I have to draw the line at Snoop Dogg."

Out of Sync

Seeing the success of boy bands in the 1990s, Lou Pearlman, who was in the helicopter taxi and blimp business, founded the Backstreet Boys and *NSYNC. His business model, however, was just another Ponzi scheme, getting new investors to pay off the money put in by earlier ones. Pearlman eventually pleaded guilty to fraud and money laundering and is serving a 25-year sentence. He now organizes the prison choir.

*Fur*rari

"*Cat*ch us if you can."

Aristo*cat* Becomes Jailbird

Lord Brocket, a polo-playing friend of Prince Charles, was jailed in 1996 for an insurance scam he'd made claiming that four vintage cars were stolen from the aristocrat's ancestral home, Brocket Hall. The cars, said to be worth millions, were three Ferraris and a 1960 Maserati Tipo Birdcage—a car *purr*ticularly popular with fat cats. But the authorities discovered that no burglary had taken place: Brocket had simply buried the cars in the grounds of his home.

Fur of a Kind

"When it comes to the gaming tables, my favorite is bacca*cat*."

Midnight Gambler

A bank manager in Biggin Hill, Kent, Great Britain, was jailed in 2014 for stealing $265,000 (£183,000) from his elderly customers to fund his Internet gambling addiction. Glenn Mason, 56, plundered the accounts of nine pensioners, including an 83-year-old woman and a 92-year-old man. He attempted to cover up his crime by transferring money using the identity of two colleagues at his branch of the NatWest bank, which led to them being fired and charged with fraud, before Mason's guilt was established.

When Payload Hits Paydirt

"Siphoning? Me? I can't even spell the word."

The Buck Stops at the Truck Stop
In 2016, a federal grand jury in Knoxville, Tennessee, indicted eight former and current Pilot Flying J employees—including the former president—for allegedly cheating customers at its truck stops out of promised discounts and rebates. Instead, it is alleged, the money went toward lining the staff members' pockets and enriching the company. Following raids by FBI and IRS agents in 2013, Pilot paid out $170 million (£117 million) in fines and settlements.

Catatonic

"I can guarantee you a *paw* return on your investment."

Carbon Credits Turn Noxious
A cheat who conned investors out of more than $100,000 (£69,000) spent the money on the good life, including gambling, buying diamonds, and living it up in restaurants and hotels. Claiming that he was investing in carbon credits, Daniel Burgoyne, a 24-year-old who lived with his mother and worked from a business park in Folkestone, Kent, Great Britain, managed to con 18 people. He invested a little more than $14,000 (£9,700) of the money he'd received. In 2015, he was jailed for two years.

The Dentist Wears Prada

"Actually, I'm more into kitten heels."

By Tooth and Claw

Joyce Trail, a 51-year-old dentist in Birmingham, Great Britain, was jailed for seven years in 2012. She had filed more than 7,000 invoices to the National Health Service for work that was never done—including fitting false teeth on patients who were actually dead. She had never seen many "patients," merely getting their names from nursing homes. The money she extracted from the NHS was spent on Caribbean vacations, Prada clothes, and Jimmy Choo shoes.

Porsche Perk is the Cat's Pyjamas

"My other car's a *Cat*illac."

Pet Stop

At a time when Pembrokeshire Council in South Wales, Great Britain, revealed that it would have to make savings of $29 million (£20 million) over two years, it was paying its head $1300 (£900) a month to lease a Porsche Panamera. Bryn Parry-Jones led the council for 18 years, becoming the highest-paid official in Wales. After being repeatedly accused of abusing taxpayers' money, he suffered a vote of no confidence in 2014 and left the council—taking with him a golden good-bye of £280,000 ($406,000).

Definitely Off Trail

"I'm as pure as the driven snow. That does mean snow you have driven through, right?"

Slippery Slopes

A company boss and her husband were jailed for milking their business in a $1 million (£690,000) fraud while their staff were being laid off. And when the staff were told that they were losing their jobs, company director Jean Murray-Shelley was away on a skiing vacation. MJL Group Ltd. supplied financial services to small companies. To sustain their lifestyle in a £1.6 million ($2.3 million) manor house in South Wales, Great Britain, as well as Harrods shopping trips and private schools for their children, Mrs Murray-Shelley and her husband Philip bled the company dry of up to $1,400 (£965) per day in cash.

The Wolf of Wall Street

"Without my glasses on, I look just like Leonardo Di*Cat*rio."

Cat Warms Itself in Boiler Room
Wolf of Wall Street Jordan Belfort went to prison in 1999 for his boiler-room stock fraud. His scam resulted in his clients losing approximately $200 million (£137 million). But Belfort is certainly a cat with more than one life. After his 22 months inside, he launched a second career as a motivational speaker—with a portion of his income going toward his restitution agreement—and his autobiography was made into a hit film. In it, Leonardo DiCaprio played Belfort not as a thieving villain, but as a roguish hero.

Meow-ow-ow

"Are you feline drowsy yet?"

Take a Price Hike

In September 2015, Turing Pharmaceutical raised the price of its drug Daraprim by 5,000 percent. Used to treat parasitic infections such as toxoplasmosis, which can be transferred by cats, Daraprim had been available at $13.50 (£9.28) per pill but would now cost $750 (£515) per dose. Unsurprisingly, there was much public *cater*wauling. Before the fur could settle on this story, Turing's 33-year-old CEO, Martin Shkreli, resigned and was later arrested on securities-fraud charges related to his employment before Turing.

Cat Burglar

"And you thought you'd never see a cat on a $100 bill."

Waste not, Want not

Wayne Kevin Jackson didn't need to be a cat burglar to steal AUS $1.2 million ($862,300 or £592,500) from Australia's Reserve Bank. Jackson was employed at the bank's printing facility north of Melbourne, where he was responsible for incinerating damaged bank notes. But rather than burn all the notes, he turned the furnace off when his colleagues left, gained access to the padlocked bags of cash, and took the money. He spent his loot on a Mercedes car, Rolex watches, and gold nuggets. Ultimately, his behavior roused the suspicion of colleagues, his theft was uncovered, and he was convicted.

The Emperor's New Catsuit

"Working for an energy firm meant I always had enough gas to cook the books."

Skilling's Killing

Jeffrey Skilling transformed Enron in the 1990s from a pipeline operator into a global energy-trading giant. But in August 2001, he unexpectedly resigned as CEO, soon selling almost $60 million (£41 million) of his stake in the company. Three months later, Enron filed for bankruptcy. With 20,000 employees losing their jobs, it was the largest bankruptcy in U.S. history at the time. Skilling had set up accounting schemes to hide the company's debts and cash-flow problems. Skilling, along with Enron chairman Kenneth L. Lay, was convicted for fraud.

Welcome to My Hotel California

"Look, if those people had never had surplus funds to invest, they'd never have lost out. Rather than spending it recklessly and damaging themselves with excessive behavior, I did that for them. Not that I get any gratitude."

Ponzi Puss

James Lewis made a living swindling the elderly of California out of $311 million (£212 million). Instead of investing their savings, he used the money as a Ponzi scheme and spent it on the good life of large homes, luxury cars, and girlfriends. Finally, the FBI caught up with him, and in 2006, the 60-year-old was sentenced to 30 years. Even with nine lives, a cat of his age might not outlive that term.

The Tail of the Banana King

"What can I say, your honor, I slipped on a banana skin."

Fermenting Pension Pots
A fruit importer, who branded himself "The Banana King," was convicted in Manhattan in March 2016 of embezzling about $750,000 (£512,000) from his colleagues' retirement accounts. Thomas Hoey, who worked for the Long Island Banana Co., siphoned money from the profit-sharing accounts of his coworkers to pay for drugs, meals, vacations, and trips to strip clubs.

Running a Bar Tabby

"I'll pass on the chips, but high steaks sound good."

Singapore Sling

In April 2004, Chia Teck Leng, a married finance manager at Asia Pacific Breweries in Singapore, was sentenced to 42 years in jail for fraud. Over four years, he had swindled banks out of $85 million (£58 million) to feed his gambling addiction. Forging colleagues' signatures, he used the cover of his business trips to gamble in Australia, Britain, and across Southeast Asia. He was so popular in some casinos that the owners would fly him over in their private jets, while he spent his winnings on lavish gifts for friends and his girlfriend.

Cat Masters Abacus

"I really got my teeth into the credit crunch. Well, someone had to do well out of it."

Hedging Cat Lands on Feet

Crispin Odey, a London-based hedge-fund manager, paid himself $41 million (£28 million) after successfully anticipating the 2008 credit crunch. That said, in 2015, his success began to fade, with his primary fund, Odey European Inc., losing 12.8 percent. By April 2016, he had gone from being a billionaire to a millionaire when his personal fortune plummeted by $293 million (£200 million) after profits tumbled at his company.

Pirouetting Puss

"Ballet has always been a passion for me. I can really get my teeth into *Swan Lake*."

Supermarket Checks out Ballet

A supermarket boss raided the store's charity fund to prop up his boyfriend's ballet company. Based in Leeds, Great Britain, Paul Kelly, Asda's vice president of corporate affairs, convinced the Asda Foundation Charity to hand over $258,000 (£176,000). He claimed that he would use it to help flood victims. Instead, the money was passed to Murley Dance Company, which was run by Kelly's boyfriend David Murley. Pleading guilty to fraud, in 2016, Kelly was sentenced to three years in jail.

Chick Feed

"In my family we have a saying: Never count your chickens until you've had your lunch."

Public Purse, Private Pocket

Should a dovecote be something politicians can claim on their expense reports? Or the costs of cleaning a moat? Or lighting a Christmas tree? In 2009, a Freedom of Information request to see politicians' expenses revealed widespread abuse of public money by Britain's Members of Parliament. The worst cases led to four jail sentences for false accounting, while others were ordered to repay money. Some, such as Sir Peter Viggers, the MP who'd requested charging his dovecote to his expenses, quietly chose not to stand for re-election.

Cat Breaks Bank

"Look at me, I'm as interested in futures as you are."

Turning Tail

In 1995, Nick Leeson's fraudulent, unauthorized derivatives trading caused the collapse of Barings, Britain's oldest merchant bank. In his first year for Barings in Singapore, he made the bank $14.6 million (£10 million)—10 percent of their annual profit—and was rewarded with a bonus of $190,000 (£130,000). But his luck soon soured, and he began hiding bad trades in error accounts. Having unsuccessfully made increasingly risky trades to try to recoup his losses, Leeson fled. Three days later, with losses at $1.4 billion (£955 million)—twice the bank's available trading capital—Barings was declared insolvent.

The Name's Bond, Junk Bond

"I'm Chairman Meow of the board."

Tangled Fur

Taking advantage of loosened U.S. financial restrictions in the 1980s, banker Charles Keating made risky investments with depositors' money. In 1986, it was found that Keating's business, Lincoln Savings and Loan Association, had $135 million (£92 million) in unreported losses and had surpassed the regulated direct investments limit by $600 million (£408 million). When Lincoln failed three years later, it cost the U.S. federal government more than $3 billion (£2 billion), and 23,000 customers were left with worthless bonds. Keating served four years for fraud, racketeering, and conspiracy.

Dethroned and Declawed

"Fat cat, you say, well, in that case, I'm leaving all my money to my dog." Leona Helmsley left $12 million (£8.2 million) to her dog, but after her death, the fund was reduced to $2 million (£1.4 million.)

Taxing Evasions

The empire of real estate multi-millionaires Leona and Harry Helmsley began to crumble when contractors remodeling one of their homes sued the couple for $8 million (£5.5 million)—the value of the building costs that the couple had failed to pay. Then, during legal proceedings in 1985, it was revealed that the building work was being billed as business expenses to the couple's hotels, which prompted a criminal investigation. Harry was too frail to stand trial, but Leona was convicted of income tax evasion.

Fur Real

"Some cats are more equal than others."

More Than a Touch of Mink

While the people of Romania were struggling to keep warm and feed themselves during massive energy and food shortages in the 1980s, their Communist dictator Nicolae Ceausescu and his wife, Elena, were enjoying a notoriously extravagant lifestyle. Apart from the o*purr*lence of their residence, Ceausescu was said to have worn a new suit every day, while the couple's wardrobes included gold-thread bathrobes, crocodile-skin bags, leopard-skin purses, snakeskin shoes, and mink furs. After the Ceausescus were executed in 1989, many of their clothes were donated to a Romanian leper colony, the last in Europe.

Fat Cat Feathers Nest

"I did not have 3,000 pairs of shoes, I had 1,060."
— Imelda Marcos.

Martial Paw

Imelda Marcos, former First Lady of the Philippines, once owned more than 1,000 pairs of shoes. Her 175-piece art collection included works by Michelangelo and Botticelli. She and her husband, Ferdinand Marcos, whose dictatorial rule included nine years of martial law, were accused of plundering their country to fund their lavish lifestyle. However, she claimed that her fortune came from finding a treasure trove of gold hidden in the Philippines by the Japanese during World War II.

A Lickety-Split Flit

"I've always been very generous with other cats' money."

Time to Flea

Owner of small American insurance companies, Martin Frankel used investors' money not to buy government bonds, as he claimed, but to take over more insurance businesses and fund his lavish life of cars, furs, personal staff, and jewels. When his con began to unravel, Frankel converted $10 million (£6.8 million) to diamonds, chartered a plane to Rome, and tried to disappear. After four months, FBI agents tracked him to a hotel in Hamburg, Germany. In 2004, he pleaded guilty to conspiracy, racketeering, securities fraud, and wire fraud.

Sweeping it Under the Carpet

"I'll take you to the cleaners. Promise."

Pulling the Rug

Barry Minkow began his carpet-cleaning business, ZZZZ Best, from his parents' garage when he was 15. Despite running up fraudulent credit-card charges, the business expanded, albeit into a Ponzi scheme where it defrauded banks, claiming that it was an insurance-restoration firm. Nevertheless, in 1985, when Minkow was just 21, ZZZZ Best went public at a value of $110 million (£75 million). Two years later, though, his scam was exposed, and he went to jail for defrauding investors. On his release, he became a pastor and antifraud agent, but in 2011, he was found guilty of stock-market manipulation.